STRAIGHT TALK ON

*Stress*

STRAIGHT TALK ON

# *Stress*

Overcoming Emotional Battles
with the
Power of God's Word!

JOYCE
MEYER

NEW YORK   BOSTON   NASHVILLE

Unless otherwise indicated, all Scripture quotations are taken from *The Amplified Bible* (AMP). *The Amplified Bible, Old Testament,* copyright © 1965, 1987 by The Zondervan Corporation. *The Amplified Bible, New Testament,* copyright ©1954, 1958, 1987 by The Lockman Foundation. Used by permission.
Scriptures marked KJV are taken from the *King James Version* of the Bible.
Originally published as *Help Me I'm Stressed*

Warner Books Edition
Copyright © 1998 by Joyce Meyer
Life In The Word, Inc.
P.O. Box 655
Fenton, Missouri 63026
All rights reserved.

Warner Faith

Time Warner Book Group
1271 Avenue of the Americas, New York, NY 10020
Visit our Web site at www.twbookmark.com.

Warner Faith® and the Warner Faith logo are trademarks of Time Warner Book Group Inc.

Printed in the United States of America

First Warner Faith Printing: October 2002
10 9 8 7 6 5

ISBN: 0-446-69148-8

LCCN: 2002115539

# CONTENTS

———⁂———

# CONTENTS

STRAIGHT TALK ON

*Stress*

# INTRODUCTION

———————∽———————

*T*hose who believe in Jesus live *in* the world but are not *of* the world. (See John 17:14,15.) This is good news for us as believers living in today's stress-filled world!

People in the world are under such intense pressure, they are often hurried, rude, short-tempered and frustrated. They experience financial and marital stress and the stress of raising children in a changing and uncertain world. Because of mental stress on the job and physical stress from overwork and frayed nerves, some people appear to be time bombs on the verge of explosion!

We as believers do not need to succumb to the stress affecting people "of the world"—people who do not know Jesus as Savior and Lord. We do not have to operate in the world's system by thinking, talking and acting like the people of the world. In fact our attitude and approach should be entirely different from the world's.

We are to be lights in the darkness. (Matthew 5:16; Ephesians 5:8.) It is hard for us to be lights, though, if we are as stressed as the people in the world! God has provided ways for us to live without being affected by that type of stress.

I have learned something in my own pursuit of peace: To enjoy peace, rather than living under the pressure of stress, I must choose in every situation to obey the Lord.

Jesus is the Prince of Peace! Obedience, or following the leading of the Holy Spirit, will always lead us to peace and joy, not to anxiety and frustration. Through God's Word we can learn more about the Prince of Peace and the inheritance made available to us by Him. We can find and maintain peace and avoid or overcome stress.

As you read this book, allow the Holy Spirit to speak to you and lead you into living in the wonderful peace of the Lord.

*Part One*

———✎———

# IS JESUS EXALTED
# OR ARE YOU EXHAUSTED?

# 1

֍

# EXCEEDING
# REASONABLE LIMITS

*Do you not know that your body is the temple (the
very sanctuary) of the Holy Spirit Who lives within
you, Whom you have received [as a Gift] from
God? You are not your own,*

*You were bought with a price [purchased with
a preciousness and paid for, made His own]. So
then, honor God and bring glory to Him in your
body.*

1 Corinthians 6:19,20

# I

⤫

# EXCEEDING
# REASONABLE LIMITS

$\mathcal{T}$he word "stress" was originally an engineering term used to refer to the amount of force that a beam or other physical support could bear without collapsing under the strain.

In our time, the word has been expanded to refer not only to physical pressure but also to mental and emotional tension.

As human beings, you and I are built to handle a normal amount of stress. God has created us to withstand a certain amount of pressure and tension. The problem comes when we push ourselves beyond our limitations, beyond what we were intended to bear without permanent damage.

For example, a chair is built to be sat upon. It is designed and constructed to bear a certain amount of weight. If it is used properly, it will seemingly last forever. But if it is overloaded beyond its capacity, it will begin to wear or even break down completely under the strain.

In the same way, you and I were designed and created to bear a certain amount of physical, mental, and emotional strain day after day. The problem arises when we allow ourselves to come under more weight than we are capable of supporting.

Everyone is under stress. Stress is a normal part of everyday life. As long as we keep that stress within reasonable limits, there is no problem. But when we allow it to exceed its reasonable limits, trouble begins.

A few years ago, I went to see a doctor because I was constantly sick. It was with one of those diseases you hear about that no one can determine what is wrong. But the doctor told me the symptoms were the result of being under stress!

When he said that, I was aggravated. I did not believe my problem was stress! I used to handle situations by throwing stressful, emotional fits, but had now grown into a fairly calm person. So being told I was under stress upset me! I thought, "You, doctor, are giving me stress!"

also result from concentrating intently on something for a long period of time.

For example, our son David works for my husband, Dave, and me in our ministry. In the past he worked on computers and designed flyers; his job was primarily mental.

One time he commented that when he got home in the evening after a long day's work, he felt as though there was a film over his eyes and a fog over his brain. For a while he felt as if he couldn't think right.

Was his body telling him he was working too hard? No, not necessarily. It simply meant his body was sending him the message, "I am moving into overload now; let me rest."

When our bodies are giving us the message to rest, instead we often push and push into greater overload. However, many times if we would just sit down, get quiet and do something peaceful for even fifteen minutes, we would feel refreshed. Our bodies have an amazing ability to rebuild and renew themselves and return to normal pretty quickly.

But if we refuse to give our bodies the rest they are calling for, we are asking for trouble. Pushing our bodies

I went to several different doctors who told me the same thing. One told me I was too intense. That *really* aggravated me to be told I was sick because I was too intense! I thought I had successfully redirected my intense nature in a positive way by working intensely for the Lord.

After a while I realized what the doctors were telling me was true. I *was* under stress. I was working too hard and not sleeping right or eating properly. I was pushing myself harder and harder—and all in the name of doing the work of Jesus! I was doing the work I had determined He wanted me to do without actually seeking Him to find out which work *He* wanted me to do, *when* He wanted me to do it and *how much* of it.

In my particular case, I was under stress because I was doing an excessive amount of all kinds of "good works"— church work and other activities related to spiritual things. I was going to Bible studies and prayer meetings. I was counseling people. I was running from one seminar to the next, preaching sometimes twenty or twenty-five times a month.

Besides the physical strain I was placing on my body, I was fighting the mental pressure of learning to run a new ministry with all the challenges involved. I was also dealing with the emotional tension that goes along with having a family and a ministry.

As a result, I was constantly having headaches, backaches, stomachaches, neck aches, and all the other symptoms of stress. Yet I would not recognize or admit that I was under stress so that I could deal with it.

You may be pushing yourself beyond your physical limits as I was. If we abuse ourselves in the name of doing Jesus' work by pushing our bodies beyond God's intentions, we will suffer results similar to the ones we would if we were exhausting our bodies in the pursuit of wealth, fame, success or any other goal.

As we saw before, everybody has some stress. None of us can get through the day without experiencing stress of one kind or another. In handling or overcoming stress, it is important to recognize it for what it is, learn how to control it and make it work *for* us rather than against us.

## Thermal Stress

From my doctor visits, I learned some interesting information about stress. There are many kinds of stress. For example, the body experiences thermal stress when it goes from one temperature to another.

One doctor explained: "If it is 90 degrees outsid you leave your air-conditioned house, run out thr the heat to the curb, jump into your air-conditione and wait for it to cool off, your body is experiencing tic change. Downtown you get out of your coc and run through the heat again on your way into ί conditioned building. From the air-conditioned buί you hurry back out into the heat to the parking lot jump back into your car and start up the air-condi You travel home in relative comfort, then rush from ί through the heat into an air-conditioned house. A change in temperature puts pressure on your bod called thermal stress."

Just as thermal stress places a strain on the p body, so mental stress places strain on the mir nerves.

## Mental Stress

Mental stress comes from trying to figure *everythi* from worrying, from thinking about the same thί and over without making any progress toward a s and from allowing the mind to run on and on by ς on little deceptive thoughts inspired by the deví into overload and continuing to push and push as if we are Superman (or "SuperChristian") will cause something to give, physically, sooner or later.

If I start to sit down in a chair and hear the legs crack, I had better take my weight off the chair fast so that I won't end up on the floor! However, many people end up in a state of exhausted collapse because they do not heed the telltale warning signs in their bodies just as severe as the legs cracking on that chair!

I hear young people say things like, "Oh, I can eat anything I want, go without much sleep for days, and it doesn't bother me a bit."

If you are a young person repeatedly pushing your body beyond its physical limits, you may continue on this way for quite a while and feel great. But you may, and probably will, severely damage yourself. All of a sudden, one day your body will say, "I can't do this anymore," and something in your body or mind will break down or become ill.

Pushing your body to the point of damage, by not supplying it with the rest and food God created it to have, is disobedience. Your body can become severely damaged as a result of this disobedience. Of course, God is the

Healer and He is merciful, but after years of disobeying Him, you may find it more difficult to receive your healing. Believe God for a lifetime of divine health while you're healthy, and add to your believing, obedience to God's laws of health. The Bible teaches us to eat properly, get good rest and not be lazy—to get physical exercise.

## Physical Stress

Physical stress occurs simply because our bodies get tired. That is normal! We are supposed to get tired. It feels good to be able to crawl into bed and get a good night's sleep after a good day's work.

However, it does not feel good to keep going and going no matter how tired we are, then fall into bed, restlessly lying there with our mind working overtime. We are adding mental or emotional stress to the physical stress.

I used to come home from long ministry trips every weekend worn out. I didn't sleep very much while gone because we worked hard and lived in changing conditions. Each night we were in a different hotel and a different bed. I prayed for people until late at night, then got up early the next morning to start ministering again.

When I went on those weekend trips, my body was

under a lot of strain because I was not able to treat it properly while we were gone. But I made the mistake of getting up on Monday morning and heading right back to the office as if I had been off all weekend.

I don't do that anymore. Now I take time off to be with the Lord. I sit in His presence and spend time with Him getting myself built back up again. Then after being renewed, I am able to do what I am supposed to be doing—what He wants me to do.

## Medical Stress

Sometimes if I exhaust myself physically and get a virus or a cold, I slow down or take some time off to rest. But the minute I start feeling a *little* better, I go back to work full force. Then I get tired or have a relapse and wonder why! I call this "medical stress."

Dave tries to tell me, "Take it easy for a while. Your body is still under strain because you haven't been feeling well. You may need to go to bed a little early for a week or two or get a little extra rest in the evening."

But like so many people, because I have things to do, I just keep pushing myself even though it is causing me physical damage.

Of course, when sickness tries to come on Dave or me, we immediately pray for healing. But if you become sick as a result of running your body down by pushing it beyond the limits God set for you to operate in good health, you need rest as well as prayer to restore your health. The boundaries He has set for us are for our own good. If we disobey by going outside of those boundaries, we open ourselves up to suffer the consequences. The body will not operate properly if it is repeatedly pushed beyond its capabilities. As previously stated, God is very merciful, but repeated disobedience can also cause us to "reap what we have sown." (Galatians 6:8.)

## Prudence

> I, Wisdom [from God], make prudence my
> dwelling, and I find out knowledge and discretion.
>
> Proverbs 8:12

A word you don't hear very much teaching about is one the book of Proverbs discusses: **prudence** (or being **prudent**). *Prudence* means "careful management: ECONOMY."[1] In the Scriptures "prudence" or "prudent" means being good stewards or managers of the gifts God has given us to use. Those gifts include time, energy, strength and health as well as material possessions. They include our bodies as well as our minds and spirits.

Just as each one of us has been given a different set of gifts, each of us has been given a different ability to manage those gifts. Some of us are better able to manage ourselves than are others.

Each of us needs to know how much we are able to handle. We need to be able to recognize when we are reaching "full capacity" or "overload." Instead of pushing ourselves on over into overload to please others, satisfy our own desires or reach our personal goals, we need to listen to the Lord and obey what He is telling us to do. We must follow Wisdom to enjoy blessed lives.

Nobody can remove all the stressors, the things causing or increasing stress, in our lives. For that reason, each of us must be *prudent* to identify and recognize the stressors that affect us most and learn how to respond to them with the right action. We must recognize our limits and learn to say, "No!" to ourselves and other people.

## Stressors

Anything can become a stressor.

For example, going to the grocery store and becoming upset by high prices may be a stressor for you.

Then the process of paying for your groceries may become a stressor. The checker in your lane runs out of change in the register and has to shut down. You switch into a new lane and learn you have selected five items which don't have prices on them. The checker has to call for a price check on each one while you wait, and the line behind you grows.

Another stressor could be your car conking out and stopping in the middle of traffic.

If the stressors are not managed properly, one by one they can mount up to bring us to the breaking point. Because we may not be able to eliminate or reduce many of the stressors in our lives, we must concentrate on reducing their effects on us. We must learn to obey Romans 12:16 and adapt: ". . . readily adjust yourself to [people, things]." When we can't control all of our circumstances, we can adapt, or adjust, our attitude so that we don't let them pressure us.

**Fight or Flight**

The human body is constructed so that any time it senses fear or danger, it reacts defensively.

For example, if you are driving down the street and see that another vehicle looks as though it is about to collide with yours, without any conscious thought on your part your body will go into action. It will automatically take defensive measures, such as secreting adrenaline, in preparation to meet that crisis situation or to avoid it.

This reaction is what professionals refer to as "fight or flight." Your body is preparing you to stand and face the situation—to fight—or to escape from the danger.

In either case your body is reacting inwardly in ways of which you may not be fully aware. Those reactions, obviously, are causing stress on your system.

**Imagination Is As Powerful As Reality**

For as he thinks in his heart, so is he. . . .

Proverbs 23:7

Something very interesting about this fight or flight phenomenon is that you do not have to be in an actual threatening situation for your body to react. Just thinking or dreaming about, imagining, or even remembering such a situation can cause your body to produce the same physical, mental, and emotional responses.

Have you ever been lying in bed late at night and heard some little noise that caused your mind to start playing games with you? You are lying there in safety and security, yet you begin to perspire, your mouth becomes dry, your heart starts pounding and so forth.

Isn't it amazing that just the mere *thought* of danger can produce exactly the same reaction as real danger? We can see why the Bible warns us of the tremendous importance and impact of our thoughts and emotions on our everyday lives!

Another example would be in hearing a vague rumor of some possible layoffs at work. When people hear that type of rumor, they usually start worrying. Some people worry to the point of having stomach trouble. The rumor has had the same effect on them as would the actual fact, yet the rumor is nothing but imagination.

The power of the mind, of thought, of imagination and emotion is immense and every bit as real as the power of the physical realm. We should make every effort not to worry, become fearful or mentally re-live situations that have been emotionally upsetting to us.

## The Results of Stress

Every frightening or stressful situation we face brought on by our mind or emotions has the same effect on our bodies as a real crisis situation.

I've read several descriptions of what happens to the body when it reacts to a stressful situation. The stressor, whatever it may be, causes an impulse to be sent to the brain. The brain combines, integrates, emotions with reasoning. With this process, the person reacting to the stressor analyzes the situation. If he perceives it as threatening, his body continues the "fight or flight" response.

The nervous system responds in three ways. It directly stimulates certain organs—the heart, muscles and respiratory system—with electrical impulses to cause a quick increase in heart rate, blood pressure, muscle tension and respiration. It signals the adrenal medulla, a part of the adrenal gland, to release the hormones adrenaline and noradrenaline, which alert and prepare the body to take action. This reaction begins a half-minute after the first, but lasts ten times as long.

The nervous system also stimulates the hypothalamus in the brain to release a chemical that stimulates the pituitary gland. The pituitary gland releases a hormone causing the adrenal glands to continue releasing adrenaline and noradrenaline and to begin releasing cortisol and corticosterone, which affect metabolism, including the increase of glucose production. This third, prolonged reaction helps maintain the energy needed to respond in a threatening situation. Nearly every system of the body is involved, some more intently than others, in the response to the stressor.

Every time we become excited, stimulated or upset, even though we may not realize it, our entire system is gearing up for either fight or flight to defend itself from the perceived threatening or dangerous situation.[2]

Then when we calm back down, our body comes out of that emergency state and begins functioning normally, in the way it is supposed to function most of the time.

The next time we face a stressful situation or become upset, the whole process starts over. Then when we calm down, the body settles back into functioning normally again.

And so it goes, up and down according to our changing mental and emotional state. But the effects of that excessive stressing and unstressing can have long-lasting and far-reaching consequences.

## Tied up in Knots?

A rubber band has an amazing ability to be stretched to its maximum length then return to its precise original form. But how many times can it do that without becoming weakened or even breaking?

When I am working in my office and break a rubber band, I tie the ends back together because I need to use it to put around something. Sometimes in our daily lives, we stretch ourselves beyond what is reasonable and bearable until we snap like that rubber band. Then we try to "tie the ends back together" and go on with the same behavior that causes us to stretch and stretch and break again.

When a rubber band I have tied breaks again, it usually breaks in a different spot, so I tie the ends together in another knot. When we keep stretching and breaking and "tying the ends together," we feel as though we are tied up in knots inside and out!

We might like for the solution to be to get rid of the causes of the problems tying us up in knots, but the source of stress is not really difficulties, circumstances and situations. A major source of stress results from approaching problems with the world's perspective rather than with our perspective as believers in Jesus Christ, the Prince of Peace.

Jesus left us with His peace.

> Peace I leave with you; My [own] peace I now give and bequeath to you. Not as the world gives do I give to you. Do not let your hearts be troubled, neither let them be afraid. [Stop allowing yourselves to be agitated and disturbed; and do not permit yourselves to be fearful and intimidated and cowardly and unsettled.]
>
> John 14:27

Jesus never said we wouldn't have to deal with anything disturbing or disappointing. John 16:33 says: ". . . In the world you have tribulation and trials and distress and frustration. . . ." But He *did* say He would deliver us out of all our afflictions! (Psalm 34:19 KJV.) John

16:33 begins, ". . . in Me you may have [perfect] peace and confidence."

John 16:33 ends with:

. . . but be of good cheer [take courage; be confident, certain, undaunted]! For I have overcome the world. [I have deprived it of power to harm you and have conquered it for you.]

Even though we will have disturbing things to deal with, we can have Jesus' peace because He has "overcome the world" and "deprived" the world of its "power to harm" us. He left us with the power to "stop allowing" ourselves "to be agitated and disturbed"! Peace is available, but we must choose it!

### The Power of the Lord

Jesus sent the twelve disciples and seventy others out two by two into every place He was about to go. Before they left, He told them: "Go your way; behold, I send you out like lambs into the midst of wolves" (Luke 10:3). But He had equipped them for the opposition they would encounter. After they returned and reported ". . . even the demons are subject to us in your name!" (v. 17), He said:

> Behold! I have given you authority and power to trample upon serpents and scorpions, and [physical and mental strength and ability] over all the power that the enemy [possesses]; and nothing shall in any way harm you.
>
> Luke 10:19

What He was saying to them is also for us today. In so many words He said, "What you are about to do will not be easy. There will be problems to face. But you do not need to be agitated and disturbed! I have given you the authority, power, strength and ability you need to overcome the power of the enemy, and nothing will defeat you—if you handle things the right way."

# 2

~

# THE KEY
# TO RELIEVING STRESS

*. . . now we serve not under [obedience to] the old*
*code of written regulations, but [under obedience*
*to the promptings] of the Spirit in newness [of life].*

Romans 7:6

# 2

⁖

# THE KEY
# TO RELIEVING STRESS

*If you will listen diligently to the voice of the Lord
your God, being watchful to do all His command-
ments which I command you this day, the Lord
your God will set you high above all the nations of
the earth. . . .*

*And the Lord shall make you the head, and not
the tail; and you shall be above only, and you shall
not be beneath. . . .*

Deuteronomy 28:1,13

When I began to prepare this message on stress, I asked
the Lord to show me how He wanted me to present the
material. I could have approached the subject many different ways. The answer He gave me, I believe, is a message, a

word, from the heart of the Father for the Body of Christ for this hour, this season.

That word is *obedience*.

The Lord said to me, "If people will obey Me and do what I tell them to do, they will not be under stress."

We may have stress, but we will be on *top* of it, not *under* it. There is a big difference between being *under* stress and being *on top* of a situation!

Jesus came to destroy the works of the devil. (1 John 3:8.) Jesus was given all "authority," "power," "in heaven and on earth" (Matthew 28:18) and has made that "authority and power" over the power of the enemy available to us (as we saw in Luke 10:19).

Ephesians 6:12 tells us, "we are not wrestling with flesh and blood" but against "the spirit forces of wickedness in the heavenly (supernatural) sphere." Verse 11 instructs us how "successfully to stand up against [all] the strategies and the deceits of the devil." Jesus has given us power to stop the devil's attacks on us.

However, nobody can stop from happening every situation that carries the potential to cause our "hearts" to "be troubled." All of us have things come our way we don't like. But, with the power of God, we can go through those situations stress free. We can be on top, "the head, and not the tail," "above only" and "not be beneath" in every situation coming our way.

Even though, like the people in the world, we will sometimes experience stressful times, if we are obedient to God's Word, and to His promptings, we can be on top of stress and not under it. We will live *in* the world without being *of* the world.

## The Major Importance of Minor Obedience

But thanks be to God, Who in Christ always leads us in triumph. . .

*2 Corinthians 2:14*

Do you believe that God is leading you into a place of victory and triumph, not into a place of defeat? Your answer as a child of God and believer in Jesus Christ would be yes! It would make sense, then, that if we believers would listen to everything the Lord tells us and obey Him, we would not get into that state of defeat, would we?

However, when many Christians hear the word "obedience," they immediately think the Lord will ask them to give away a huge sum of money, move to Africa to go on the mission field or do something else really big they don't want to do! They don't realize that obeying the Lord usually involves some minor thing that will make a major difference. Obeying Him in the *little* things makes a *major* difference in keeping stress out of our life.

Simply obeying the promptings of the Holy Spirit will often relieve stress quickly, while ignoring the promptings of the Holy Spirit will more than likely cause stress *and* cause it to increase equally quickly!

### The Promptings of the Spirit

But now we are discharged from the Law and have terminated all intercourse with it, having died to what once restrained and held us captive. So now we serve not under [obedience to] the old code of written regulations, but [under obedience to the promptings] of the Spirit in newness [of life].

Romans 7:6

According to this passage, we are no longer under the restraints of the law but now serve the Lord under obedience to the promptings of the Holy Spirit. A prompting is a "knowing" down on the inside of you telling you what to do. First Kings 19:11,12 describes the "still, small voice" the Lord used with Elijah.

> . . . And behold, the Lord passed by, and a great and strong wind rent the mountains and broke in pieces the rocks before the Lord, but the Lord was not in the wind; and after the wind an earthquake, but the Lord was not in the earthquake;
>
> And after the earthquake a fire, but the Lord was not in the fire; and after the fire [a sound of gentle stillness and] a still, small voice.

A prompting from the Lord is not like hitting someone over the head with a hammer to "prompt" them to do something! The Lord did not use the great and strong wind, the earthquake or fire as a prompting, but instead came as "a sound of gentle stillness" and "a still, small voice."

A prompting as "a still, small voice" is not necessarily a voice, but can be God's wisdom giving you direction in that moment. First Corinthians 1:30 tells us, ". . . But it is from Him" [God] "that you have your life in Christ Jesus, Whom God made our Wisdom from God. . . ." If we are born again, Jesus is living inside us. If He is inside us, we have God's wisdom in us to draw on at any moment! But unless we *listen* to wisdom, it won't do us any good.

Since a prompting is very gentle, it is easy to question whether it is from God, and it is also easy to completely ignore it. One time when I was shopping at the mall, after I had been there for three or four hours, I heard a prompting from the Holy Spirit which said, "You need to go home now." I had been able to purchase only half of the eight or so items on my shopping list, so I ignored the prompting.

The remaining items on my list were not immediate needs. Even though the prompting of the Spirit within me told me to stop what I was doing and go home, like many determined goal-oriented people, I was *not* going to leave until I purchased every item on my list.

I had come for eight items, and I was leaving with eight items! I didn't care if I had to be dragged bodily out of the mall, I was going to leave with what I had come to buy!

I had reached the point of being so tired and upset I wasn't thinking clearly beyond, "I just want to finish and get out of here!" Simply being civil any time anyone asked me anything was becoming extremely difficult. I can't remember how many times I've done that to myself—pushing beyond the prompting of the Holy Spirit. And because of the state I've brought on myself, I even start an argument with Dave. A telltale sign of being on overload is if we are no longer displaying the fruit of the spirit—love, joy, peace, patience, kindness, goodness, faithfulness, gentleness and self-control—Galatians 5:22,23 tells us about.

I could have simply obeyed the prompting of the Holy Spirit, that "still, small voice," and by going home, relieved the stress from the situation. Instead, I moved ahead in my own fleshly determination to achieve my goal and brought stress on myself and everyone around me!

## God's Anointing Is on Obedience

God's grace and power are available for us to use. But God enables us, or gives us an anointing of the Holy Spirit, to do what *He* tells us to do. Sometimes after He has prompted us to go in another direction, we still keep pressing on with our original plan, while actually asking Him to help us do what He said not to do! "God, help me—I'm so close to finishing—Lord, just help me do a little more, and I'll be done!" If we are doing something He has not approved, He is under no obligation to give us the energy to do it.

We are functioning in our own strength, rather than under the control of the Holy Spirit, because we are doing something God has told us not to do! Then we get so frustrated, stressed or burned out, we lose our self-control, as I did at the mall, simply by ignoring the prompting of the Spirit.

I believe a major reason many people are stressed and burned out is from going their own way instead of God's way. They end up in stressful situations when they go in a different direction from the one God prompted. Then they burn out in the midst of the disobedience and, struggling to finish what they started outside of God's direction, beg God to anoint them.

God is merciful, and He helps us in the midst of our mistakes. But He is not going to give us strength and energy to disobey Him continually. We can avoid many stressful situations and living "tied up in knots" simply by obeying the Holy Spirit's promptings moment by moment.

## God Blesses Obedience

Sometimes God *does* give direction requiring major change. He *does* tell some people to go on the mission field in Africa or to give away large sums of money. But God created the body of Christ with different abilities, strengths and desires to reach people in many different ways. (1 Corinthians 12.) Jesus came that we might "have and enjoy life, and have it in abundance (to the full, till it overflows)" (John 10:10).

God loves you and wants to bless you abundantly. (Ephesians 3:17–20; 1 John 4:16,19.) Once you have an understanding of how great His love is, you will no longer be afraid that He will ask you to do something which would be bad for you. As we have seen, obedience to the promptings of the Holy Spirit will always lead us to peace and joy—victory, not to defeat.

When you stop to really consider it: Do you think God would ask us to obey Him in something as big as going to the mission field when He knows we have a hard time obeying Him in something as small as going home from the mall when He tells us? He works with us on our level. As we grow in obedience to minor things, He leads us into major things.

**Special Obedience**

God places specific requirements on each of us that may not make sense to anybody else. He knows what each of us needs to fulfill the plan He has for us.

Jesus was obedient to the requirements of God's plan that would enable Him to bring salvation to mankind.

Although He was a Son, He learned [active, special] obedience through what He suffered
And, [His completed experience] making Him perfectly [equipped], He became the Author and Source of eternal salvation to all those who give heed and obey Him.

Hebrews 5:8,9

A young man who works for our ministry told me of a specific requirement God gave him. Paul and his wife, Roxane, are a tremendous blessing to us both through the work they do in our ministry and also to us and our children, personally.

Paul is one of the calmest and most easygoing people you would ever want to meet. Nothing ruffles or bothers him. But Paul told me he wasn't always that way. When he gave his life to the Lord, he was just the opposite. He couldn't sit still. He couldn't stay home even for five minutes.

Paul's family told Roxane that as a child, Paul was almost hyperactive. They were amazed at his transformation after he gave his life to the Lord. The transformation resulted from Paul obeying one specific thing the Lord asked him to do.

The Lord required that Paul stay home with his family for one full year. One of the reasons for the requirement was that Paul didn't know how to be still. Asking a young man in his twenties to stay home night after night with Mom and Dad seemed almost unreasonable, but Paul knew God was leading him. Paul's obedience helped prepare him for his current ministry.

### Acknowledge the Lord

Lean on, trust in, and be confident in the Lord with all your heart and mind and do not rely on your own insight or understanding.

In all your ways know, recognize, and acknowledge Him, and He will direct and make straight and plain your paths.

Proverbs 3:5,6

One of the most important things we can learn in this day and hour is how to be still.

Although some of the time we move too slowly and most of the time we move too fast, the major problem is that we move in the flesh. We jump up and do things without acknowledging the Lord.

## Be Still and Know God

Let be and be still, and know (recognize and understand) that I am God. I will be exalted among the nations! I will be exalted in the earth!

Psalm 46:10

One of the main reasons so many of us are burned out and stressed out is that we don't know how to be still, to "know" God and "acknowledge" Him. When we spend time with Him, we learn to hear His voice. When we acknowledge Him, He directs our paths. If we don't spend time being still, getting to know Him and hearing His voice, we will operate from our own strength in the flesh. As we saw before, we can burn out because God is not obligated to anoint us in doing something He didn't direct.

We need to learn to be quiet inside and stay in that peaceful state so that we are always ready to hear the Lord's voice.

Many people today run from one thing to the next. Because their minds don't know how to be still, they don't know how to be still. At one time I didn't know how to stay home for an evening, and I was a full-grown adult!

I felt I had to find something to do every evening. I had to be involved and on the go, being a part of whatever was going on. I thought I couldn't afford to miss anything that happened because I didn't want anything to go on I didn't know about. I couldn't just sit and be still, look at a tree in the backyard or drink a cup of coffee. I had to be up doing something. I was not a human being—I was a human doing.

Our young friend Paul was like that. At the age of twenty-two he had the call of the Lord on him but didn't know what it was. Paul was so used to *doing*, the Lord required Paul to *do* only *one* thing: Stay home with his family for a year.

Even though the requirement was simple, obeying would be hard. Paul was used to running around with his friends every evening. Paul knew every night his flesh would start screaming, "I want to go out with my friends!" For Paul to obey God's requirement took special obedience.

One of the reasons the Lord told Paul to stay home for a year was to establish good family relationships. So for the next year Paul was there in the family barbecuing for them, watching good movies with them—spending time with his mom, dad, brothers and sisters. But he was still so full of his old lifestyle, he found it hard to be still. In the evening he roamed all over the house.

"I would rotate around the house at night. My mother said she saw me in the kitchen at least six or seven times a night. I just couldn't be still; I had to be up doing something."

The difference in him between then and now is amazing. It's hard to believe he was ever that way. The Lord wanted to keep Paul still for a year so that He could do the work needed in Paul. I believe if Paul had not obeyed God for that year, he would not be in the position he is in now, experiencing the blessings, including the peace and joy, that result from doing God's will.

## Prompt, Exact Obedience

One of the areas in which I have had to learn obedience to the Lord is in talking—or more precisely—in when to *stop* talking.

If you are a big talker like me, you understand why I say there is anointed-by-the-Holy-Spirit talk, then there is vain, useless, idle talk, the kind the apostle Paul warns about in his letter to young Timothy. "But avoid all empty (vain, useless, idle) talk, for it will lead people into more and more ungodliness" (2 Timothy 2:16).

There have been times when we have had guests in our home and I have finished saying what the Lord wanted me to say, but then continued talking. We can usually pinpoint the moment when what we are doing switches from being anointed by God to being *us* continuing on in the flesh—in our own strength. After that point I was rambling, really saying nothing, or repeating the same things over and over.

Sometimes when people left our house to go home, I was exhausted. If I had quit talking two hours earlier when the Lord told me, I wouldn't have been worn out from all my empty, vain, useless, idle talking!

Another time I asked the altar workers to assemble in order to give them a word of instruction about a few changes in the way we were handling the prayer lines. I talked to them for about an hour and shared with them what I had planned to say. That was fine. But then I thought of a little something about obedience and shared that, then shared about something else.

I was just about to really get on a roll, when all of a sudden Dave stood up and said, "Well, it's time to go home." He saved me from going on and on with vain, useless, idle talk. And because I had continued beyond God's prompting, *I* was starting to feel rattled.

The special requirement the Lord had for me was to learn to say what He wanted me to say, then stop.

> . . . For God sets Himself against the proud (the insolent, the overbearing, the disdainful, the presumptuous, the boastful)—[and He opposes, frustrates, and defeats them], but gives grace (favor, blessing) to the humble.
>
> 1 Peter 5:5

When we feel frustrated, we usually want to blame the devil. But the frustration we feel when we push beyond the point God tells us, happens because we are continuing on in our own strength—He has quit helping us! If God's approval is on what we are doing—whether it is shopping, doing dishes or talking—He is energizing us because He is doing it through us.

Have you ever been talking with someone about a tender subject when the discussion suddenly takes a turn and becomes a little heated? You can tell feelings are starting to get out of control and that little prompting on the inside of you says, "That's enough. Don't say any more."

That prompting, though small, is very strong, and you know saying one more thing would not be wise. But after thinking for a minute, you decide to plunge on in with the flesh! You press right on in and make your comment. A few minutes later, you're in an all-out war!

I used to do this when Dave and I started to discuss something, and without stopping to think, began tossing slightly heated comments back and forth. Immediately the Holy Spirit would quicken me with that little prompting inside, "Don't say another word."

I would think, "One word? Just one more word won't be that bad. Surely one more word won't get me in much trouble!" After I would plunge on in with the "one more word," I was always reminded of the importance of prompt, exact obedience! I discovered from Dave's reaction I couldn't have picked a worse thing to say if I had tried! I was also reminded of the Lord's special requirement for me to say *only* what He wants me to say and no more.

When we say something after the "still, small voice" prompts us to stop, and the person we speak to reacts, later we often ponder over the whole incident, baffled. We say, "God, I don't understand what happened!" "What happened" is so simple and can be avoided so easily: God told us to do something and we disobeyed. The minute we disobeyed, His anointing lifted and the frustration began. In the situations above, if we had obeyed the promptings and kept quiet, things probably would have settled back down, even in five minutes. Then the Spirit would have let us know it was all right to continue that conversation.

Sometimes all we need is a little break just to let things said, settle. But because the prompting is so small, it's easy to think, "Oh, it won't make any difference if I just say *this*," and press on in the flesh. The prompting is so slight, pushing ahead in spite of it doesn't seem like disobedience, but that's exactly what it is!

We soon discover how much difference disobeying the "still, small voice" made! The minute the Spirit says, "That's enough," we need to stop. If we keep going, we are asking for frustration and defeat.

If He says, "Don't say another word," He means exactly that. Sometimes we have our own version of obedience. We interpret a prompting like that from the Lord to mean, "Don't say another *word*. But if you want to say two or three *sentences* more, that's fine"!

When we realize that continuing on beyond the Lord's prompting even just a little is moving into disobedience, we are able to understand "what happened"—His anointing lifted; therefore, frustration was able to immediately come in. We are also able to understand why obeying the Lord's promptings in the small things is so important.

### Five Minutes of Obedience

Recently when I was studying extremely hard, I was becoming very tired mentally. A little prompting said to me, "Just get up and walk away from it. Take a five-minute vacation."

A few years before, I would have pushed on ahead in order to make sure I covered the amount of material I had set as my goal. But instead, I obeyed the Holy Spirit's prompting! I went downstairs, walked around a bit, talked to my daughter, drank something, stretched a little and looked out the window for a few minutes. When I felt ready again, I went upstairs and dived back into my studies—refreshed!

Just five minutes of obedience relieved the pressure and stress building in me. If I had ignored the prompting and continued studying until I reached my goal, my studying wouldn't have been as fruitful. And I would have probably been exhausted and irritable!

If we keep pushing, the work we do from the point we disobey will not compare in quality to the work we would have produced under the Holy Spirit's anointing.

# 3

⁓

# SET UP FOR BLESSING

*Samuel said, Has the Lord as great a delight in
burnt offerings and sacrifices as in obeying the
voice of the Lord? Behold, to obey is better than
sacrifice, and to hearken than the fat of rams.*
                                    1 Samuel 15:22

# 3

⌒⟍⟋

# SET UP FOR BLESSING

When God prompts us to do little things, He is never trying to take anything away from us. He is always trying to set us up for a blessing.

He prompted me to go home from the shopping mall that time knowing I was heading into overload and about to display anything *but* the fruit of the Spirit! If from the beginning I had slowed down and quieted my mind enough to hear His promptings, He could have shown me which mall stores to look in for the items I needed. I could have finished my shopping trip in thirty minutes *and* in peace!

Things the Lord asks us to do which look unimportant to us are apparently very important from His point of view! Once we fully understand the importance of hearing and immediately obeying the Lord's promptings, we will want to set as a priority doing what we need to do to stay in a place of peace, ready to hear.

### ". . . That It Might Go Well with Them . . ."

Deuteronomy 5:29 states:

> Oh, that they had such a [mind and] heart in them always [reverently] to fear Me and keep all My commandments, that it might go well with them and with their children forever!

If we will simply *listen* to the Lord and *do* what He says, things will go well for us. To bring the result God intends, we need to add action to the hearing.

Our young friend Paul had to add action to the Lord's instructions for him to stay home for a year in order for the result the Lord wanted, to come to pass. It was hard for Paul to obey the Lord's particular requirement for him, and the process took some time, but the Lord was setting him up for blessings! Because Paul was obedient, the result was total transformation!

Often the Lord wants us to spend a little time with Him so that He can refresh us. At night many people sit down in front of the TV because they're tired. Then when they sense the Holy Spirit prompting, "Turn it off and come away with me," they don't realize the Lord is trying to set them up for a blessing!

They say, "Lord, you know I work all day. I would like to just relax a little bit in front of the TV."

If they are in that state, they are not relaxing! Usually, the longer they sit there, the more tired they become. But by obeying the Lord, even ten minutes in His presence can bring the refreshing they are trying to find by watching TV.

I don't mean to imply watching TV to unwind is a bad thing. Sometimes I like to make popcorn, get something to drink and watch a good movie on television with my family—just relax. The point I'm making is how important it is to obey the Lord's promptings.

While I'm sitting there watching the movie, the Holy Spirit may prompt me, "Come upstairs for half an hour." The problem would be if I thought, "But, God, I prayed this morning," and disobeyed the prompting! It may have been one of those times when I thought, "It can't make that much difference if I watch this movie with my family and spend some time with the Lord later." If I continue watching, usually the movie is one I don't enjoy. Then I go to bed frustrated, thinking, "Oh, I just wasted the whole evening."

Instead I could have immediately responded to the Lord's prompting by saying to my family, "Excuse me—I'll be back." After spending half an hour with the Lord, I would have come back with His peace all over me and could have easily heard any promptings He was giving me to change the channel to a particular movie we would enjoy much better!

## Simply Obeying God

Most people have no idea how simple it is sometimes to relieve stress, and Satan works to keep it that way! He works to complicate people's lives in every imaginable way because he knows the power and joy simplicity brings.

Satan wants to exhaust the energies God has given us by keeping us too busy and stressed out trying to handle all the things complicating our life. He knows that if we learn to simply obey God, we will turn that power and energy against him by hearing and doing the work God directs!

The transformations many people desire in different areas of their life come through forming a pattern of obeying God in the little things. He may ask you to come away and visit with Him for half an hour or an evening instead of watching television, going to a party or talking on the phone. The more consistent you are in keeping yourself still enough to hear His voice, then obey His promptings, the sooner the needed work will be done in you for the transformations to be complete. God uses our obedience in the little things to transform our life.

No matter what the situation, listen to the Lord and obey. As we saw before, Proverbs 3:6 states: "In all your ways know, recognize, and acknowledge Him, and He will direct and make straight and plain your paths." You may not understand the reasons the Lord asks you to do particular things or see any changes or results immediately, but keep obeying the Lord and things *will* go well with you and your children!

## Obedience Is Better Than Sacrifice

First Samuel 15:22 says, "to obey is better than sacrifice. . . ." There are times we must make sacrifices in true obedience to the Lord, but sacrifices we make as a result of moving out in the flesh will lead to stress. We may "work hard for God" according to *our* ideas of what we should do for Him rather than taking time to be still in order to hear *Him* tell us what *He* wants us to do.

When we "work for Him" in the flesh, we sacrifice time the Lord really desires to use in another way, and we may also sacrifice our health, peace and the quality of our relationships, as we saw before.

If we continue on with what the Holy Spirit prompts us to do after He tells us to stop, we *will* sacrifice because doing the work without His anointing won't be easy! However, God will never abandon us (Hebrews 13:5), and He continues to work with us in the midst of our wrong choices.

Even if we make a wrong choice and are functioning in our own strength, we may still accomplish some things for God. According to Romans 8:28 KJV, ". . . all things work together for good to them that love God, to them who are the called according to his purpose."

We need to remind ourselves we aren't perfect. We won't always make the right choice, do the right thing or obey God perfectly every time. We all make mistakes and when we do, the only thing we can do is ask God to forgive us and go on.

But by obeying God, we will accomplish *specifically* what He wants done at the time and in the way He wants it done, which promotes peace instead of stress. Through obeying the Lord, we place ourselves in position for Him to be able to bless us in the way He desires and plans.

The Prince of Peace, Jesus, Who lives inside those of us who have received Him, knows and will reveal to us the specific actions we need to take in every situation to lead us into peace. He also knows what we need to do in order to prepare for what He has planned for us.

The particular requirements He places on each of our lives may not make sense to anybody else or even to us at the time! But once we understand how much God loves us and fully comprehend that everything He asks us to do is to take us up into a higher level of blessing, we will want to abandon ourselves to Him in trust! As a priority, we will want to keep ourselves in a place of peace to be able to hear and respond immediately to Him.

He may prompt you to go home from the shopping mall to keep you from becoming exhausted, irritable and hard to get along with. He may tell you to zip your lip because he knows you are about to say something you will wish you hadn't! He may ask you to obey Him by stopping what you are doing, to get up, walk away and take a five- or ten-minute vacation to relieve pressure building up and to refresh you. Or He may ask you to come away and be still in His presence for half an hour.

## Exalt Jesus

Relieving stress—leading a peaceful, happy life, free from exhaustion and burnout—does not need to be complicated!

It is helpful to have a general understanding of the physical effects of stress and important to have a spiritual understanding of the source of stress and the solution to relieving it through Jesus. But we don't need to learn all the details of the medical causes and cures or go into a deep theological study of stress to be relieved of it!

The Lord told me if we will begin to exalt Jesus, we won't be exhausted. If we will begin to exalt Jesus by giving Him first place in our everyday lives, the place of preeminence, through listening to Him, obeying Him and doing what He shows us to do, we won't be exhausted.

We may lift up our hands and say, "We exalt You," but we are truly exalting the Lord when we obey Him in everything He asks.

The apostle Paul mentions "the simplicity that is in Christ" (2 Corinthians 11:3 KJV). There is a wonderful simplicity available to us through Jesus. Relieving stress is simple: Obey the promptings of the Holy Spirit. Obey *immediately*. Do exactly what the Lord says to do, no more and no less.

You can probably think of specific areas in your life in which obedience to small things God is telling you to do would relieve a great deal of stress. I think you will be quite amazed to discover that by beginning to apply this principle of immediately obeying the prompting of the Holy Spirit, a week later you will be able to say you experienced less stress than you did the week before.

When you feel like that rubber band all tied up in knots stretched out to the point of breaking again, take a deep breath and remember: Jesus left us His peace. He gave us the power to be on top of stress and not under it. We can live in the world and not be of it by drawing on the power of the Prince of Peace, listening to His voice and responding with prompt, exact obedience to live peacefully, happily and free from exhaustion and stress.

*Part Two*

---❧---

# Scriptures to Refresh the Weary, Build Strength, Relieve Stress, Prevent Stress

# Scriptures
## to Refresh the Weary,
## Build Strength, Relieve
## Stress, Prevent Stress

*In* this section, Scriptures are grouped together to use in practical application to everyday life.

## *To Relieve Stress*

### Receive Power and Strength from the Lord

When we are tired, the Lord can strengthen and refresh us. He will refresh our body and soul.

Sometimes when I'm ministering to a very long prayer line, I can feel myself just starting to cave in physically and even mentally. I stop for a second and inside I say, "Lord, I need help here—I need You to refresh me." And as the

Scripture promises, He increases my strength, causing it to multiply and making it to abound.

If you are sitting at your desk or cleaning your house; if you have worked all day then need to go home and cut the grass or change the oil in the car, the Lord can refresh you. Lean back for a minute and let Him give you that power.

> Have you not known? Have you not heard? The everlasting God, the Lord, the Creator of the ends of the earth, does not faint or grow weary; there is no searching of His understanding.
>
> He gives power to the faint and weary, and to him who has no might He increases strength [causing it to multiply and making it to abound].
>
> Isaiah 40:28,29

The Lord can renew your strength.

> Even youths shall faint and be weary, and [selected] young men shall feebly stumble and fall exhausted;

But those who wait for the Lord [who
expect, look for, and hope in Him] shall change
and renew their strength and power; they shall
lift their wings and mount up [close to God] as
eagles [mount up to the sun]; they shall run and
not be weary, they shall walk and not faint or
become tired.

Isaiah 40:30,31

## Come to Me, All You Who . . . "Have Burnout"!

The answer to burnout is spending time with God. No
matter how much material you read or how many semi-
nars you attend on stress, you will find the relief you want
from stress and burnout by going to God and letting God
refresh your soul.

The Lord will give rest to the overburdened. In other
words, the Lord will give rest to the burned-out!

Come to Me, all you who labor and are heavy-
laden and overburdened, and I will cause you to
rest. [I will ease and relieve and refresh your souls.]
Matthew 11:28

The Lord is my shepherd; I shall not want.

He maketh me to lie down in green pastures:
he leadeth me beside the still waters.

He restoreth my soul. . . .

Psalm 23:1–3 KJV

The Lord's burden is to be light and easy to carry. We
take *His* yoke upon us by obeying His promptings.

Take My yoke upon you and learn of Me, for I am
gentle (meek) and humble (lowly) in heart, and
you will find rest (relief and ease and refreshment
and recreation and blessed quiet) for your souls.

For My yoke is wholesome (useful, good—
not harsh, hard, sharp, or pressing, but comfort-
able, gracious, and pleasant), and My burden is
light and easy to be borne.

Matthew 11:29,30

Enter into the Lord's rest by believing, trusting and
relying on Him.

For we who have believed (adhered to and trusted
in and relied on God) do enter that rest, in

accordance with His declaration that those [who did not believe] should not enter when He said, As I swore in My wrath, They shall not enter My rest; and this He said although [His] works had been completed and prepared [and waiting for all who would believe] from the foundation of the world.

Hebrews 4:3

## Enjoy Your Life

The thief comes only in order to steal and kill and destroy. I came that they may have and enjoy life, and have it in abundance (to the full, till it overflows).

John 10:10

And now I am coming to You; I say these things while I am still in the world, so that My joy may be made full and complete and perfect in them [that they may experience My delight fulfilled in them, that My enjoyment may be perfected in their own souls, that they may have My gladness within them, filling their hearts].

John 17:13

## *To Prevent Stress*

### Use Wisdom

Your body is the temple of the Holy Spirit.

> Do you not know that your body is the temple
> (the very sanctuary) of the Holy Spirit Who lives
> within you, Whom you have received [as a Gift]
> from God? You are not your own,
>    You were bought with a price [purchased
> with a preciousness and paid for, made His own].
> So then, honor God and bring glory to Him in
> your body.
>
> 1 Corinthians 6:19,20

The Lord gives power to the faint and weary; but remember, if you are worn out from continually exceeding your physical limitations, you need physical rest. The Lord may mercifully give you supernatural energy in particular instances, but you are in disobedience when you abuse your body, the temple of the Holy Spirit. As we have seen, the anointing lifts when you operate outside of God's promptings.

If you want God to flow through and work through you, you need to take care of your body so that God can use you. If we wear out the body we have, we don't have a spare in a drawer somewhere to pull out!

## Take a Sabbath Rest

It is important to take a Sabbath rest because we need certain periods of time to just let go of all the usual things we do and think about. We need to spend time with God to restore our energies and let Him restore our soul.

You may not take your Sabbath on Sunday. It may be Saturday or Friday, or a half day on Tuesday and Thursday. The issue is not what day to set aside but to definitely set aside a certain portion of time in which to just totally and completely rest and relax.

> Six days you shall do your work, but the seventh day you shall rest and keep Sabbath, that your ox and your donkey may rest, and the son of your bondwoman, and the alien, may be refreshed.
>
> Exodus 23:12

## Obey God in Making Commitments

Commit only to those things the Lord tells you to do, and say no to the others. You only have so much energy. If you don't use it doing the things God has told you to do, you will run out and have none left to use in the things you should be doing.

To release God's anointing on your life, find out what He wants you to do, then make your yes be yes and your no be no. In other words, stick to what you know in your heart is right for you.

> Let your Yes be simply Yes, and your No be simply No; anything more than that comes from the evil one.
>
> Matthew 5:37

Be a God-pleaser—not a man-pleaser.

> Now am I trying to win the favor of men, or of God? Do I seek to please men? If I were still seeking popularity with men, I should not be a bond servant of Christ (the Messiah).
>
> Galatians 1:10

## Stay Calm

Blessed (happy, fortunate, to be envied) is the man whom You discipline and instruct, O Lord, and teach out of Your law,

That You may give him power to keep himself calm in the days of adversity, until the [inevitable] pit of corruption is dug for the wicked.

Psalm 94:12,13

Do not fret or have any anxiety about anything, but in every circumstance and in everything, by prayer and petition (definite requests), with thanksgiving, continue to make your wants known to God.

And God's peace . . . which transcends all understanding shall garrison and mount guard over your hearts and minds in Christ Jesus.

Philippians 4:6,7

Casting the whole of your care [all your anxieties, all your worries, all your concerns, once and for

all] on Him, for He cares for you affectionately
and cares about you watchfully.

1 Peter 5:7

## Promote Peace in the Way You Live

And the servant of the Lord must not be
quarrelsome (fighting and contending). Instead,
he must be kindly to everyone and mild-
tempered [preserving the bond of peace]; he
must be a skilled and suitable teacher, patient
and forbearing and willing to suffer wrong.

He must correct his opponents with courtesy
and gentleness, in the hope that God may grant
that they will repent and come to know the Truth
[that they will perceive and recognize and
become accurately acquainted with and
acknowledge it].

2 Timothy 2:24,25

Live in harmony with one another; do not be
haughty (snobbish, high-minded, exclusive),
but readily adjust yourself to [people, things]

and give yourselves to humble tasks. Never overestimate yourself or be wise in your own conceits.

Romans 12:16

Fathers, do not provoke or irritate or fret your children [do not be hard on them or harass them], lest they become discouraged and sullen and morose and feel inferior and frustrated. [Do not break their spirit.]

Colossians 3:21

### Trust the Lord

He who dwells in the secret place of the Most High shall remain stable and fixed under the shadow of the Almighty [Whose power no foe can withstand].

I will say of the Lord, He is my Refuge and my Fortress, my God; on Him I lean and rely, and in Him I [confidently] trust!

Psalm 91:1,2

Trust (lean on, rely on, and be confident) in the Lord and do good; so shall you dwell in the land and feed surely on His faithfulness, and truly you shall be fed.

Psalm 37:3

# Prayer to Combat Stress

—⟨∽⟩—

*Father,*

*I set as my priority spending time with You to hear Your voice clearly and to obey You. Help me to keep my priorities in order.*

*I know that as I place You first by spending time with You, You will cause me to do supernaturally all the things I need to do.*

*I know that You want me to have peace in every area of my life and have made that peace available to me. I thank You that when we ask for wisdom, You give it to us. I ask that You guide me and give me wisdom so that I know clearly the commitments to make.*

*I thank You, Lord, that I use my energies in the way You want them used. In Jesus' name I pray, amen.*

# PRAYER FOR A PERSONAL RELATIONSHIP WITH THE LORD

───────⟡───────

*I*f you have never invited Jesus, the Prince of Peace, to be your Lord and Savior, I invite you to do so now. Pray the following prayer, and if you are really sincere about it, you will experience a new life in Christ.

*Father*

*You loved the world so much, You gave Your only begotten Son to die for our sins so that whoever believes in Him will not perish, but have eternal life.*

*Your Word says we are saved by grace through faith as a gift from You. There is nothing we can do to earn salvation.*

*I believe and confess with my mouth that Jesus Christ is Your Son, the Savior of the world. I believe He died on the cross for me and bore all of my sins, paying the price for them. I believe in my heart that You raised Jesus from the dead.*

*I ask You to forgive my sins. I confess Jesus as my Lord. According to Your Word, I am saved and will spend eternity with you! Thank You, Father. I am so grateful! In Jesus' name, amen.*

See John 3:16; Ephesians 2:8,9; Romans 10:9,10; 1 Corinthians 15:3,4; 1 John 1:9; 4:14–16; 5:1,12,13.

# ENDNOTES

Chapter 1

1. *Webster's II New College Dictionary* (Boston/New York: Houghton Mifflin Company, 1995), s.v. "prudence."

2. Compiled from the following sources: H. R. Beech, L. E. Burns and B. F. Sheffield. *A Behavioural Approach to the Management of Stress.* Ed. Cary L. Cooper and S. V. Kasl. Chichester: John Wiley & Sons, 1982, pp. 8, 9 and 11.

   Randall R. Cottrell, "The Human Stress Response," in *Grolier Wellness Encyclopedia: Stress Management,* 1st ed. (Guilford: The Dushkin Publishing Group, 1992), V. 13, pp. 34, 35.

   *Webster's II,* s.v. "adrenal gland," "endocrine gland," "pituitary gland."

**JOYCE MEYER** has been teaching the Word of God since 1976 and in full-time ministry since 1980. She is the best-selling author of more than sixty inspirational books, including *In Pursuit of Peace, How to Hear from God, Knowing God Intimately,* and *Battlefield of the Mind.* She has also released thousands of teaching cassettes and a complete video library. Joyce's *Enjoying Everyday Life* radio and television programs are broadcast around the world, and she travels extensively conducting conferences. Joyce and her husband, Dave, are the parents of four grown children and make their home in St. Louis, Missouri.

*To contact the author write:*

Joyce Meyer Ministries
P. O. Box 655
Fenton, Missouri 63026
or call: (636) 349-0303
Internet Address: www.joycemeyer.org

*Please include your testimony or help received from this book when you write. Your prayer requests are welcome.*

To contact the author
in Canada, please write:
Joyce Meyer Ministries Canada, Inc.
Lambeth Box 1300
London, ON N6P 1T5
or call: (636) 349-0303

In Australia, please write:
Joyce Meyer Ministries—Australia
Locked Bag 77
Mansfield Delivery Centre
Queensland 4122
or call: 07 3349 1200

In England, please write:
Joyce Meyer Ministries
P. O. Box 1549
Windsor
SL4 1GT
or call: (0) 1753-831102

BOOKS BY JOYCE MEYER

*Battlefield of the Mind*
*Battlefield of the Mind Study Guide*
*Approval Addiction*
*Ending Your Day Right*
*In Pursuit of Peace*
*The Secret Power of Speaking God's Word*
*Seven Things That Steal Your Joy*
*Starting Your Day Right*
*Beauty for Ashes* Revised Edition
*How to Hear from God*
*How to Hear from God Study Guide*
*Knowing God Intimately*
*The Power of Forgiveness*
*The Power of Determination*
*The Power of Being Positive*
*The Secrets of Spiritual Power*
*The Battle Belongs to the Lord*
*Secrets to Exceptional Living*
*Eight Ways to Keep the Devil Under Your Feet*
*Teenagers Are People Too!*
*Filled with the Spirit*
*Celebration of Simplicity*
*The Joy of Believing Prayer*
*Never Lose Heart*
*Being the Person God Made You to Be*

*Me and My Big Mouth!*
*Me and My Big Mouth! Study Guide*
*Prepare to Prosper*
*Do It Afraid!*
*Expect a Move of God in Your Life . . . Suddenly!*
*Enjoying Where You Are on the Way to Where You Are Going*
*The Most Important Decision You Will Ever Make*
*When, God, When?*
*Why, God, Why?*
*The Word, the Name, the Blood*
*Tell Them I Love Them*
*Peace*
*The Root of Rejection*
*If Not for the Grace of God*
*If Not for the Grace of God Study Guide*

JOYCE MEYER SPANISH TITLES

*Las Siete Cosas Que Te Roban el Gozo (Seven Things
That Steal Your Joy)*
*Empezando Tu Día Bien (Starting Your Day Right)*

BY DAVE MEYER

*Life Lines*